Firedamp

poems by

SUE ALDRED

Copyright Sue Aldred 2009

All rights are reserved.

ISBN 978-0-9556868-5-6

Acknowledgements and thanks to Cliff Ashcroft, Phil Ilsley, Kim Simmonds-Hurn, Ann Copeland, and all the members of Poetry-ID, Letchworth, Adele Salem, Graham Fawcett, and i.m. Julia Casterton. To ArtemisPoetry where the poem Felt was published.

Special thanks to Stephen Wyatt, Mark Heines, and to Ed Aldred for his unfailing love and support.

Contents

Spark	11
Pigs rooted for them	12
Now as I was young	13
Blockhouse	15
Coal clichés	16
Frosted Glass	17
Splinters	18
Felt	20
Fog	21
Moon-watch	22
Secrets	23
Runaway	24
Dead Troops Talk	25
Firedamp	26
Some mothers' sons	27
If you came to me	28
First Love	29
Dough	30
Turning	31
Orange	32
Handprint of a stillborn son	33
Pinks	34
Fairground Horses	35
Dacha in August	36
Pushkin Mall	37
Pilgrimage	38
In the fishing shack	39
Surrender	40
Fire Instructions	41

Spark

When I was young my indigo

was a reverb of the heat of the sun,
dreamed in June dust,
in dry fields and between the cracks
in stones where I came to thrive.

I was alive. And I had a calling
to give out my colour and scent.

Now I am faded to paler shades,
two-hued memories of stinging blue.
And I am dry, drier than tinder.
Drier than cork oaks on the side of the hill.

Like them, with a spark I will burn.

Pigs rooted for them

in mother's day. I chose carefully,
making the choosing seem like wealth.
The fresh sweet scent of them
changed in the roasting
to bitter. Still we agreed

it came nowhere near.
It was ersatz,
it made us sullen
and long for parcels,
food-hoard from Canada.

To taste that acorn brew
was insult to the tongue
that called it coffee,
which came, we knew, in bottles,
the hedonistic liquid dark as tar.

Later, we were craven, we did not
refuse. We smiled, smacked our lips,
sucked it through our teeth,
sighed.

Now as I was young

Now as I was young and flying into the out-of-doors
tearing from me the tight and eyeless helmet of rust
        and rectitude, with a faint buzzing
            sound of unspoken longings,
                and as I was young in calling and called
by all in me that was green, awake and forcing my way
lightwards like wild wheat, the garden's threshold rolled
        me down its bank to where prairie lay,
            tumbling grasses grazed by buffalo.

And as I was free and knowing who had won the War
As well as I knew the time I could tell from blowing
        the parachute seeds of dandelion,
            my tank gouged craters in gravel
                and the concrete shelter stood guardian,
who could have known better than I, despite its smell of pee,
how much more kindly it claimed my restless imagining
        than the punishing certainties
            that propelled me clear of the house.

For home was driving me, home with its hearth of insult
urging me out with my squad lined up ready for kick-off
        to leap for headers, dive for penalties,
            shoot from free-kicks and corners,
                until shouldered at last with the Cup
I was hailed triumphant, hurrayed as heroine and cheered
on my victory circuit, high with applause of the crowd,
        cartwheeling somersaults of joy
            at the turning of shame to glory.

And as I was ancient and heavy with knowing my youth,
Nunkie and Heidi both on the lush wide summer pasture,
    arabesquing on the running board,
    Ford Eight cresting the ruts,
    or balanced brave on pedal blocks
of the cross-barred bike too big even for my long legs,
I was fearless, Calamity Jane on my Deadwood Stage
    a-rollin' on over the plain,
    six-gun primed for the coming attack.

Now across my dream field and its caves and crevices,
pigeons flutter at dusk back to kits of fancying miners
    with news from black streams in distant woods
    to this wilful post-war baby:
    ghost riders on the sunset ridge
halt with spears, solemn as stars in the deepening blue.
They make no promise to guide me on my flight of innocence,
    shield me from century's rain:
    they sing only of leaving, leaving.

Blockhouse

Four walls, roof of concrete, low
enough, and flat for climbing on.
War games' perfect emplacement.
Then the thought, no door:

why would they build it like this?
No sign of one made then blocked up.
We circle, hand over hand, twice round,
then notice the pigeon holes

under the eaves, two black squares.
Heat shimmers, shadows lengthen.
If I were one of the circling swifts
I could fly inside, and look.

Coal clichés

Coal clichés my critic called them,
and advised me to steer clear.
A year ago it was, and I obeyed.

These are the clichés: men in thousands
dragged with bare hands at black rock.
That bare, that black, are clichés.
Thousands, dragged
are the words that must be shunned.

The winding-gear is gone. The silver rails
don't gleam in the rain now.
We must not mention them for they embarrass us
more than the dark Satanic mills.
A cliché that my father's lungs
and my grandfather's and his father's
were wrecked getting their living.
The words for their fight for breath
to be avoided, their hot vapour
too close upon our necks.

What have they done to you, white-faced millions,
you ancestors? Does shame keep you underground?
You formed the guts and sinews
of a machine now ghostly in us. Madness
and suicide we inherit, not silicosis.
What have they done to you, you carcasses,
remote now as medieval effigies?

Frosted Glass

screaming   laughing   crying at the same time
outside myself I could see through them   Mum's brain
bubbling like lava   Dad wanting to brain me but
he slammed the bedroom door
and locked it instead
                          for the damage I done

shit   toys all over the place   comics   games,
sherbet lemons exploded on the carpet
I'm not staying in this filth I said and

                    climbed out the window
                      jumped down
                      on the wheelie bin
                      that buckled a bit
                      I'm a fat git
                      walked round
                      and went back
                      in the front door

I'm back I said   I'm back

                                        faces like
                                            frosted glass
                                                  before I
                                          smash it

Splinters

Born in a rhythm not my own
that I had to learn to rock with
resisting, making cross-currents, wave-bashing,
note-crashing, whirling pools
without benefit of stave,
restless I improvised. Branches
wind-raked either bend or are battered
to pieces.

And pieces were made of me
to be collected after the storm
for firewood, kindling, kinder
than might be expected

taking me down to memory,
the wordless heartwood, grained and pulsing
that made me know I had
a bark and trunk that could be split like that.

And after the fire,
the understanding, kindly fire,
I was singing through the ash
and soot-specks, sifting
sweet air through my teeth:

and melody made its bargain
even with the compelling,
the fact of force, shutting me up
while my arguments formed
on rough lips, on bitten skin,
on blood blisters, on broken staves
of old songs and
even older
splinters.

Felt

She stranded the oily fleece
washed, not spun,
then trod it between cloths.
A small piece, to show me.

The dye she chose was blood.
She made me copy every step,
looking into my face
to make sure I knew.

I remember bony fingers
smoothing the wool,
a baby crying somewhere till
the stream's clatter soothed it.

With it my childhood fell away
trodden, then squeezed into a round
under my hands. What could I make from this?
Slippers, a cap, a child's toy.

Fog

There were mines beneath our feet.
Under the skin of old men, soot's fine tracery
in dark seams healed over.
We knew fog then: smoke from black gold
congealed in air

rimed the surfaces of bark
and brick; it lined nostril and nail
and wound its way into the narrow
shafts of lung, thickened with effort.

At fourteen we took lamps with us
in the cage warm with our breath.
Our living was turning earth inside out,
digging in dark for roots of things.

Above us heaps of slag burned dull
sullen as old grudges: chimneys pebble-
dashed with fallout from constant fires.
Their fine ash risen, crystallised
and falling earthwards turned
its attention upon us,
coating us with its vapour,
loath to leave home.

Moon-watch

"As I view the moon,
Many things come into my mind,
And my thoughts are sad".   (Oe no Chisato)

I am a green frog
lined with red. I wait for her
to spike my sadness
here on my floating tatami.

Her full round expanse
yields no words: the world listens
for wisdom, but fails
like me at human language.

Secrets

Plankton that teems in billions can be
sensed only in sussurating waves:
their wriggling and nearly silent sea
seethes in a shell's emotional architraves.

Listen. One still night with your oars at rest
lit by a slender shard of moon you'll hear
going about their stolen business, ghosts.
Is it the pull of pleasure that you fear?

Night fisherman, you will know which line to cast,
until your ears and eyes are tired at last,
your body sick of straining into the dark:
suspended like a guilty question-mark.

Runaway

The eldest girl was looking for her dad -
I'd thrown him out -

I said, don't pick an argument with me
young lady, so she went.
And it was cold. Goodwill to men. I spent
the day wrestling that fucking tinsel tree

out of the shed, telling the other kids, Mum's here,
it's going to be the same as always, you'll see.

> I had been getting on her nerves.
> Her gran got on mine when I was fifteen.
> Looking at me like I was some
> piece of dirt the cat dragged in.

She's out there now, somewhere.
I could pick the phone up. Wish I had.
That's one thing he could always do.
Reason with her, calm her down, her dad.

Dead Troops Talk
(a photograph by Jeff Wall)

In the gallery one no-brain soldier
demanding answers, points with the dried
stump of his right wrist.

> *We dance, we sing, we impersonate*
> *in a studio, not on a battlefield.*
> *We are the tableau vivant of the dead.*

A corpse swings a mouse by the tail
in front of his dead comrade:
they flaunt parody wounds.

> *We are actors in a charade.*
> *We are chanting of the home fires.*
> *Our pantomime makes light of what is deadly.*

The one on the left is trying to shake
the madness out of his skull while his mate
looks on; curious, uninvolved.

> *You dead are with us, like it or not.*
> *Having no voices of your own*
> *you follow cues we give you.*

Here in the gallery a sign says
exit: no readmission. But in the photograph
the artist has his way: he breaks the frame.

> *Don't look to us for answers.*

Firedamp

Fear me: a silent soldier
waiting for the secret spark.
My longing binds me to black walls,
slick with run-off from lost streams.

Fear me. A good son to his mother,
I cannot speak my intent.
But when your yellow bird
falls in its cage, be wary.

I am ignitable, you cannot teach me.
I will not learn. My desire smoulders
within these confines,
craving seams of fossil heat.

Prometheus was my name
when there were rational tales about me
explaining my furious yearning
that led me to steal from God.

Do not pity me, or seek
to understand. I am the firedamp
seeking to shaft your certainty
and rule you from beneath.

Some mothers' sons

The walls are black with fires of ordnance.
God knows the state of those within, robbed
of their voices. A thin wind carries only
our smell, unwashed besiegers, as often as not
caught in our own crossfire.

The dead cry for their mothers. We are in
a timeless land, the shore deserted by the sea;
our worst illusion, that high tide,
the fruitful sane cycle of city life
is permanent.

Besiegers and forgetters,
our fate is to be marooned,
full-moon-struck:
to run amok in our blood-vengeful will
to throw our lives at these gates

while the surrounded ones
keep their starved vigil,
souls white-hot with refusal.

If you came to me

If you came to me this minute and said
I want you, the shy animal would bolt
into the dark of warren or beech wood:
you will not find her. She will not be held.

And yet a glance could do it. A mere touch,
crossing the main road, or at the counter
licking stamps; the sudden taste can fetch
a sense faithful as frost in a mild winter.

Be blind, you with your seeing expertise.
I want you shaken out of your well-defined
certainty, off-centre, ill-at-ease
and not obedient to demands of mine.

First Love

      I stood without roots
      and the gale shook me -
      laughter, bonhomie -
      she's gone. My first lover.

      I gave her every cent.
      Money was easy. Bleeding
      pulp was what she took.
      She ripped the root of me, gutted me,
      slit me through the breast bone,
      reached inside and tore away
      what I never knew I owned.

I come to myself in the bar. The lads
soft-punch me in the shoulder, uncertain.

We walk home, this other she
and I, like strangers. How could she know
another woman's ghost took hold of her
when I turned at the Rugby Club door.

Dough

First a snake was made.
Then a heart that the dough
snake could twist around.

I pulled and pounded all
my disappointment into creatures,
organs, rolls of desire.

Then each piece was a lost friend;
what could I do with them,
in their pale and unbaked state?

Naked and raw, clammy to touch,
unfinished stories whose end I will never know:
in these kneaded mounds

I mourned playgroup days,
rough shapes of show-and-tell,
the stuff of growing.

I pulled them into a clump
that would be bread, the plain resource,
a lump of undeciding. Then,

crusts under my nails, I made
a plaited loaf, and left it
rising.

Turning

On her back is his resting hand.
The muscles flex in spider grip.
Is it release or ownership,
the sleeping hand that lies across
the wakeful one?

She turns, he moves away:
separate promontories.
Missing the weight of the unawake,
she cannot share his isolation,
only imagine its self-absorption.

There was a turning once they could
have taken. Their allegiance
proved stronger, like an ancient lock
with a key forged from these separations
that still can close, and open.

Orange

In the car park of the Albany
Saturday afternoon Deptford Market is winding down.
Next to the mended Dysons salvaged from a tip,
in the heat of smashing plates
she approaches

giving off rays of sunset orange,
loops of her braids above.
Pieces of crockery zing past her child's ears
and she turns her burning eyes on the vast
tattooed arms of the man flinging the useless
dishes at the skip
where unheeding shards are flying.

Bursting with citrus outrage
the fruits of her wrath, not sweet,
sharpen the man's in turn
but she is not one to back down
she with the sun on her side, until

he rolls his wheelie bin out of range
of her pelting, skin-splitting,
maternal fusillade.

Handprint of a stillborn son

Placing the dead palm on ink
then on the paper flat,
his mother registers his mark,
stamp of his almost-being.

Unblinking the child his sister
witnesses bruised, closed lids.
She takes the inkpad and with care
cushions the cold foot with it.

Watching their rite reminds me of my loss:
the brother, life unlived, the one
whose football shirt I wore
when I ran with the boys.

If I had known his handprint in a book,
would I have torn the shiny plastic limbs
like insults from my dolls, tortured
their hair, and their dead hands?

Pinks

Sleeping late I dreamed of waking, and dad was here,
his features as I knew them, not pale but his cheeks red,
as though he'd run from a distant touchline.
Grief meets me with a cool drink of water.

Always in your presence the repeated rinse and spin
of complaint would leach colour from everything. It's how
I stayed close to you, mother, thirsty in monochrome,
the homely-hateful spread of grey I look for now.

But the pinks you gave me are vibrant, edged with darker
frill: they are beating with warmth and vigour, like the pulse
of rainfall, infatuation, bloody-minded joy.

Fairground Horses

Shrieking children, delighted lovers
I carried up and down, when I had music,
when I went around.

From the bankrupt fairground
somebody cut me loose,
me and my partners

and dizziness became my element
when somebody broke up the ride,
me and my partners;

when they broke us and dumped us here,
too solid for firewood,
paint worn off long ago.

We could make our exit any day now.
We have ourselves a team still,
me and my partners

while chickens scratch around our hooves.
We wait in silence, still partners,
as we stand in our straightened rows.

Dacha in August

After the heat of the fire, the singe
of salmon and pork belly, the clouds
full of rain raced over as we ran
for cover into the dacha.

Elena and her mother inspected
the mushrooms we'd picked that morning
and cleaned them one by one
in the tiny kitchen. Natalia showed me the ladder
and I climbed up to the mezzanine.

Stretched out on the platform bed
I hovered in a drowse of voices.
Mushrooms started to sing in the enamel pot,
their warm vapour gathering around me.
Raspberries over the low flame let out their juice
scarlet with sugar for cordial.

Having no Russian, we took
black dominoes from the Navy box;
yelling, cheating, and unwrapping candy
we waited out the storm

and Sergei, deep-sea diver, beat us hollow,
with his confident Soviet smile.

Pushkin Mall

The squares in Moscow are dignified
with imposing bronzes of literature's greats.
Gogol and Dostoevsky stare down, immortalised
by the Soviet regime. Being safely dead
they could be elevated. First among these
honoured, is Pushkin, a poet.

What does it mean to write Pushkin
on a plate or in the sky? Is it
a dream full of longing
to make a world full of poets, as if
they could do a better job than politicians?

But now I hear your statue in the square, the haunt
of lovers, still a meeting point for radicals,
is threatened by another shopping mall.
European kitsch, Prada handbags, cut-glass
gold-encrusted decanters, Sheffield solid silver forks.
How about that, Pushkin? Would you care? Perhaps you loathed
the idea of glorifying artists. Chekhov did.
They stopped the show to read him speeches of praise
when he was coughing up blood. And you,

Pushkin, you jerk, got shot in some silly duel replicating
the fate of your hero Lensky. Poets. You all
go the same way in the end, you writers
that inspire us with your example. The only difference
is what you leave behind. Not just
a statue, a metro station, a street name.

Pilgrimage

My hair was told in a vision
to take herself off for a week or so
to Spain on pilgrimage
all the way to Santiago.

The going was tough on the plains
of La Mancha. She lay in sweaty strands
on the hard shoulder, the heat
shrivelling her split ends.

She sent me a postcard when
she made it. Wish you were here,
it said. Miss you, am very burnt.
I felt the cold around my ears

and wore a woolly hat till she flew in
on EasyJet, texted me from Luton:
can you collect, am in need of wash.
We sang Come Together on the way home.

In the fishing shack

She stands at the counter, staring out at the scene,
waiting. A dog rootles in shingle,
lifts its leg on the corner of the lifeboat station.
The old boy is busy sluicing knives,
all the bleached grey surfaces.

A pause
in which a lot or not much happens.

She points, he grabs the last two plaice,
bangs them in paper, wraps them tight and says
seven pounds fifty.

Somehow the skinning and the boning part
she meant all along to ask for, the gutting,
the careful attending to detail,
are lost in the look he hurls,

the look that might have said,
you confuse me with a man
who skins fish for a living.

Surrender

She wouldn't speak to the vicar
the new one from down under
who delivers her eulogy.

She wouldn't go to church any more
afraid of the plot booked in her name.
They lower her into it carefully.

She wouldn't let in the organist's wife
who brought her KitKats anyway,
and laughs about it after the burial.

She wouldn't be seen without her curls.
The vicar unlocks his Harley
from the bootscraper by the lych-gate,

the wind ruffling his ponytail
as he roars off to his two o'clock wedding.

Fire Instructions

In the secure ward Malcolm stands by the hose reel
the tubing pressed to his cheek
and gazes into the glass box
with the button inside.

> *At the sound of the bell proceed in an orderly fashion*
> *to the safety exits which you will find*

In the world he thought permanent, Malcolm
had been in charge of safety. He loved drills
and correct procedure, made sure exits
were clear and unimpeded.

> *Remove patients from the immediate vicinity*

While another resident
was causing a disturbance,
Malcolm tugged at the hose,
unwound it the length of the corridor,
returned to the alarm, and with a chair
he broke the glass.

> *Use the extinguishers provided.*
> *For a person's clothing use blankets.*
> *Leave your belongings and do not return.*

But in this demented world he would set fires,
if someone would give him a light.

www.ingramcontent.com/pod-product-compliance
Lightning Source LLC
Chambersburg PA
CBHW021028090426
42738CB00007B/942